The Next Lesson

by Dr. John Cassone

ISBN-10: 1494869020
ISBN-13: 978-1494869021

DEDICATION

I wrote this book for Siena, Bella, Maya, and Dominic. I want them to know why we're here and the purpose of the trials of life. I encourage them to break through conflict orientation to live a life of inspiration.

Contents

John Cassone, Ph.D.

This story is meant to inspire healing
on a deep level. It is metaphoric in nature
and not intended to contradict nor
oppose any particular ideology.

The term "God" is used as a symbol to
represent the Great Mystery, or what
is beyond our understanding directly but
essential to recognize personally. In this way,
the message can be useful to those
both of religious and non-religious orientations.

Part I
The Next Lesson

John Cassone, Ph.D.

Chapter One
The Soul

John Cassone, Ph.D.

In the beginning there was only Nothingness.

Perfect Nothingness.

...some call it the mind of God.

An Idea

occurred.

This Creative Idea, like all Creative Ideas, came from the Nothingness.

In other words...from the Mind of God.

And, like all Creative Ideas from the Mind of God,

it was perfect.

God created the Soul.

The Soul is a perfect expression of God. It is a creative potential designed to Love and Create just like God.

The soul, however, cannot do this by itself.

The Soul can only Love and
Create by letting God in.
In this way, the Soul Loves and
Creates through God.

The Soul by itself.

It is not Creating or Loving yet because it has not let God in.

This Soul is letting more God in.

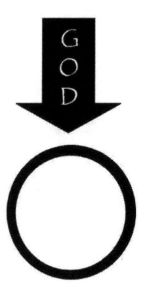

Lots of Creativity and Love

as a result of letting

more God in.

Chapter Two
The World

John Cassone, Ph.D.

Next,
God Created the World.

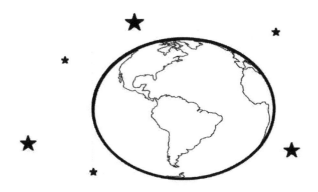

The only purpose of the World is to teach the Soul to let more God in.

The World

...and the things
of the World,

serve no other purpose.

Chapter Three
Fear

All Fear
comes from an illusion.

It is the
Great Untruth.

The World appears
separate from God.

The Soul in the World
begins to believe it
is of the World
instead of an inseparable
expression of God.

It begins to believe in the
Illusion that it is
Separate and Alone.

All Fear comes from this
Illusion. However, it is part
of the design.
Fear is one of God's
most important teaching tools.

The only way for the Soul to conquer Fear is to remember the Truth that the Separation is an Illusion and that the Soul is connected to God and, in fact, an expression of
God's Love and Creativity.

This is sometimes
Called a
Spiritual Awakening.

When the Soul enters the World and feels Fear it gets very excited and thinks it needs to do something.

This creates a paradox.

The harder the Soul tries, the more it relies on itself, the more self-centered it becomes, the more separated from God it feels, and the more Fear it feels.

New Fears arise up
because the Soul only sees a
world of Separation and Fear
and so addressing Fears
becomes its full time job.

It is exhausting.

"Me me me," cries the Soul. It has become self-absorbed as all of its efforts are focused on its own well-being.

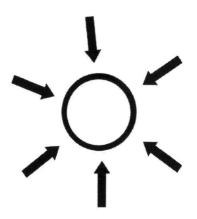

God feels far away and hardly a solution to the problems of Life.

Chapter Four
Willingness

John Cassone, Ph.D.

A Soul that is full of Fear is an Unhealed Soul.

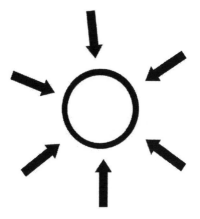

A Soul's only purpose
is to Heal, which involves the
release of Fear and the
reconnection to God, and then
to Heal other Souls that are still
Unhealed.

All Souls are meant to be Healers.

This Soul is Inspiring other Souls.

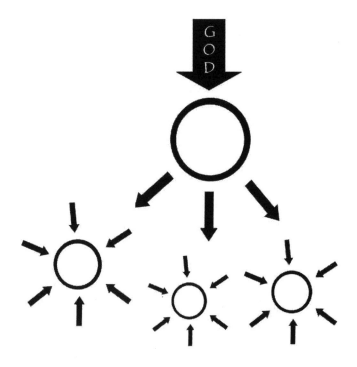

All Souls are meant to serve others still in pain. This is what it means to be a Healer.

An Unhealed Soul will use its rational mind to support its self-centeredness.

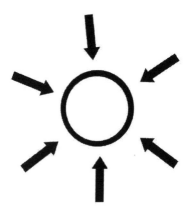

These are all stories that become a prison and must be let go of in order to Heal.

It is very painful for an Unhealed Soul to try so hard at controlling the World so that it can satisfy itself because ...it never works.

Only when a Soul has had enough pain from trying to arrange Life to suit itself will it become Willing to Let Go and seek Truth.

It is very difficult for a Soul to accept Truth (that is it lovable beyond comprehension) when it has created so many stories that seem to make sense. But when the Pain is great enough the Soul will Let Go of the stories.

Healing can happen
instantaneously as God's Love
is greater than any story.

Through God
the stories become irrelevant
...even ridiculous.

Willingness is the only requirement for the Soul to rediscover God and begin Healing.

John Cassone, Ph.D.

Chapter Five
Being Human

John Cassone, Ph.D.

When a Soul enters a human body it is still a Soul.

It is still in Truth a perfect creation connected to a limitless source of Love. The body is just a vehicle for the Soul to learn Lessons that are Spiritual in Nature.

The body was designed to trigger all of the Soul's Fears.

The body feels separate,
vulnerable, needy, and can die.

None of this is true for the Soul
but the Soul
forgets Truth and thinks
it's a body.

The Soul tries to fill itself up
with all kinds of things because
it feels so empty and fearful.

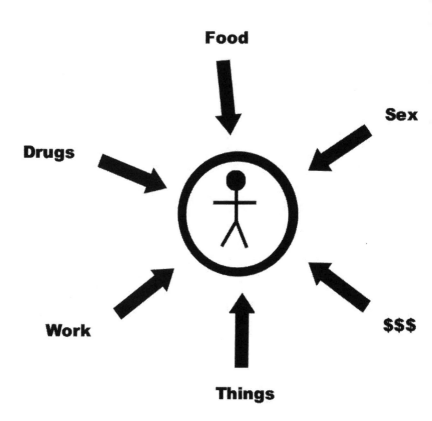

...but it is never enough.

Pain, emptiness, loneliness, sadness, anger, and all forms of discomfort only serve one purpose: to bring a Soul closer to God.

The Soul's experience as a human is supposed to be miserable at times. If it wasn't, the Soul would never seek God.

Just to make sure
the Soul doesn't get too
comfortable, God designed
another tool perfectly made to
bring about the kind of
frustration and
resentment sure to rattle a Soul
to its core.

Chapter Six
Relationships

John Cassone, Ph.D.

God created sexuality. It is part
of the plan.

Souls are Spiritual beings
having a Human Experience.
The desire for one another is
simply a tool to give
the Souls a strong need to work
out and resolve the
separation from God with each
other.

Sexuality creates a need for another Soul and the fantasy that another Soul can solve the problem of Life instead of seeking God. This is a perfect recipe for the kind of pain that eventually leads a Soul back to God.

Sexuality by itself does not mean anything. It is just biological.

...but as a lesson plan, it is priceless!

"I want you and I want you to want me!"

Souls use other Souls to try to
fill the emptiness.
They use each other like a drug
to avoid the deep feelings
of loneliness that only God can
fill. Souls even make
legally binding agreements to
ensure use of each other.

The sense of ownership
and exclusivity helps the Souls'
insecurities about getting a
steady supply of a drug-like fix
from one another.
Relationships are full of
pain and conflict as long as
they are built on taking from
each other.

An Unhealed Soul will appear to be giving to another Soul but they are only doing so to get what they want from the other Soul which is really taking instead of giving.

This principle of Fear and Selfishness is not limited to romantic relationships.

Authentic Love for our
children honors mistakes as
lessons making mistakes an act
of Healing; an act of Love.

When a parent tries to solve
their own insecurities through
their children they
are self-centered no matter
how loving they think their
efforts are. Frustration is
a key sign of a selfish act.

There is less tolerance,
understanding, or compassion
for another's approach to Life
because it threatens the World
according to them.

"I want you to be different than you are so that I feel better about Myself!" – parent says to child.

Love is the only quality of
authentic value in parenting. It
comes from God, through the
parent, and to the children.
It transcends circumstance
which is a good thing
because circumstances are
often unpleasant when
raising children.

True Love can only come from and through God.

It is not meant to satisfy the human experience but instead to set a Soul free from it. It is an expression of God and an act of Healing.

As long as one Soul is upset
at another Soul
there can be no Healing.

Every Soul that has ever yelled at, made fun of, picked on, attacked, harmed, or even murdered another Soul had a Reason.

Reasons are used to support upsets that have no reason.

This makes Reason a very poor lens from which to see the World.

It is a fantasy that another Soul can change enough to satisfy any other Soul.

...only God can do that.

The paradox of experiencing a truly Loving Relationship is that it has Nothing to do with the Relationship.

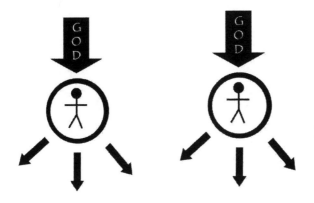

Two Souls in a relationship walking side by side in Life.

They look to God to satisfy
their individual needs instead
of each other.

This allows for Love instead of
Neediness. They are able
to focus on giving more than
taking because they
are satisfied through God.

"It's ok for you to be who you are. My identity is not dependent on you. This gives you space to make the common and clumsy mistakes we all make as Humans."

"Your shortcomings no longer frustrate me as you are not a solution nor a threat to my well-being."

Chapter Seven
One Solution

John Cassone, Ph.D.

The very same principles are involved in all the problems of the world. It's all the same lesson; physical problems, mental, emotional, relationship, financial, etc.

(far from God)   (close to God)

DARK   **LIGHT**

Compass of Light and Dark

<u>Always</u>
There is only one problem:
Separation from God.

<u>Always</u>
There is only one solution:
Connection to God.

More Self:

worry

stress

isolation

judgment (others and self)

think too much

insecurity

overwhelm

defensive

resentment

frustration

exhaustion

fear

anxiety

addictions

depression

upset

neediness

codependency

obsessing

separation

It's a full time job
playing God and running life
self-powered instead of
God-powered.

"If only everyone would just do what they're supposed to!"

<u>More God:</u>

present
spontaneous joy
meaning
purpose
passion
creativity
intuition
inspiration
loving
service
gratitude
compassion
acceptance
forgiveness
contentment
tolerance
acceptance
unity
connection

Contentment is experienced
not because cravings
and desires are satisfied but
instead because of the
connection to God.

High level contentment
is called Bliss and it is not of
this world.

Inspiration and clarity
show up without direct effort.
This is Grace.

Sin is sometimes presented as a list of behaviors or a moral code. A deeper understanding has less to do with a behavior and more to do with the intention behind the behavior.

Sin = Selfish

Love (God) = Service

In order for a Soul to move
from self-centeredness to God-
centeredness it must stop
praying for what it wants and
instead pray to let go
of what it wants.

A Soul will always know if it is Self-centered when the focus is on the Outcome.

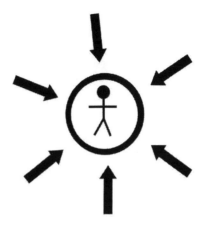

"I'll be ok when ...."

"I'm not ok because of ...."

When a Soul is God-centered it
feels ok for no reason.
It is no longer subject to the
ups and downs of this World.

This allows for the experience of Bliss.

Grace is the realm of the miraculous and it comes with a sense of awe and wonder woven into our daily experiences.

Grace is only given when the Soul stops trying so hard to get what it wants.

Hardships are supposed to happen. Approaching Life as if they are not is the source of much Conflict and Pain.

A Soul always
has a choice.

"God, allow me to let go of everything I think I know about my upset for an open mind and a new experience.

Free me from the bondage of Self that I may better serve."

Think of the problems
of Life as God knocking at your
door gently (and sometimes
not so gently) reminding you
that there are no real solutions
in the World.

In this way, all hardships are
The Next Lesson
on a Spiritual Journey aligning
us with God.

The End

John Cassone, Ph.D.

.

Part II
The Daily Practice

Instructions

This section of the book is instructional. It contains a 30 day workbook based on The Daily Practice. There are actions you must take every day and writing in the workbook is essential. These actions represent the practical use of the principles from part I of this book. They are meant to move you from conflict orientation to inspiration. It requires that you take action which is simple in nature but life changing in application.

There are three core aspects to **The Daily Practice:**

1. **Morning Intention:** set the intention for the day. Build inspiration into your life.
2. **Clean as You Go:** during the day, watch for elements of darkness and rid yourself of them immediately as they appear.
3. **Evening Soul Surgery:** take an inventory of remaining dark spots. Remove them.

The following section is a workbook called the Daily Practice. Make a commitment to completing it, without missing a single day, for a total of 30 days. This will help to solidify the principles of the daily practice internally and adjust your mindset.

Remind yourself that you are never upset for the reasons you think. We use reason to justify our upsets but our upsets are driven internally by the loss of Light; loss of God. In other words, upsets are fueled by the darkness that lives in us. Upsets show up more often and in greater intensity when we are disconnected from the Light.

The willingness to see life as a lesson plan takes the emphasis off the situational matters of life and places the focus back on our experience of growth. The goal of have less dark and more light. By following the guidance in this book, you will shift from management of the external world to management of the internal world. Treasures of the external world can be taken from you. Treasures of the internal world are untouchable.

Elements of darkness accumulate within us from based on upsets that are supported by reasons. These reasons are not facts even though they appear to be based on facts. The reasons are created to justify the upset feelings which create the darkness. It is the reasons that hold the darkness inside us which eventually strangle the sunlight of the spirit. Reasons are perception based and build false rationale structures that sustain elements of darkness. The upsets, hurt, and pains from which the darkness structures are built do not go away with time or with age. They do not go away if we suppress or ignore them. They only go away with intention directed at their removal.

The Daily Practice will teach you to identify the darkness and remove it. By following the workbook you will identify elements of darkness as they accumulate. Your daily practice will also allow for elements of darkness based on past experiences to surface, be exposed, and removed so that they no longer keep you from the light. Elements of darkness stick to us internally like residue from past events that we took personally. Factually, an event may have happened but the pain always comes from our self-centeredness which is the place within that darkness grows. We take things personally and therefore make it about us. Resentment, hurt feelings, and fears make up the sticky residue of internal darkness.

Every time a dark thought or feeling arises we have an opportunity. If we think we our reasons for being upset are justifiable and that we are right to be upset then we stay sick. The elements of darkness will continue to grow and eventually drown out the sunlight of the spirit. However, if we stop ourselves and interrupt the darkness pattern then we break the cycle. We can intentionally remove and let go of the upset regardless of our reasons. In this way, the elements of darkness will be removed and with each removal we experience greater freedom. We become more present; more light.

This requires that all throughout the day you check yourself for frustration, resentment, worry, fear, insecurity, or upset. These emotions are your tailor made lesson plan telling you exactly what to remove and when it needs removal. When they arise, it is your cue to take action. If you miss the cue and do not take action then the lesson will not be learned. It will repeat again showing up in other situations causing repeat patterns and unnecessary suffering.

We must detangle the events of the real world

from how they affect us spiritually. When upsets occur, acknowledge to yourself that there is a fact level occurrence which may or may not need to be addressed. However, because there has been a negative emotional reaction, you must prevent the situation from affecting you spiritually. You must take action in the moment to stop further accumulation of darkness. In this way, clarity regarding the situation will return and wasted efforts, based on managing emotional pain, will be reduced.

Increasing the light in us and how it shows up in our lives also requires intention. Creating a spiritual shift for a passion based life can seem like an overwhelming mission. The secret is that we only need one day. One spiritually appropriate day, where we follow the light and drop the dark, is all it takes to live a purposeful life. To heal the world we must first heal ourselves and everything starts with one day. An amazing life is simply a series of amazing single days. This is why this is called the daily practice.

By dropping the darkness we leave room for the light. We are not used to having less darkness as it used to be our full time job managing it. This is why our Daily Practice must equally place intention on cultivating the light or we risk returning to the dark. We must learn to play and create alongside the basic responsibilities required of us in real life. When we heal, we role model healing for others including family, friends, coworkers, and children. It is the design.

Heal yourself. That is your mission here on Earth.

Workbook

Daily Practice

Date: _____

Morning Intention

Today is the Day.
Today is all I have. Today is all I need.

"Free me from the bondage of self that I may live in the present and with authenticity. Allow me to be the person I am meant to be as a light shining in this world serving others still in need."

playful   creative   meaning   grateful   service

joyful   purpose   passion   inspiration

compassion   contentment   forgiveness

tolerance   loving   acceptance   intuition

integrity   honesty   loyalty   perseverance

authenticity   genuineness

Circle one of the principles above to bring in light for today. In the following lines write the actions or behaviors that you intend to do today to bring these concepts alive in your life. Keep it simple.

_____

_____

_____

_____

_____

_____

_____

Each day we have responsibilities that require our action. It is easy to add mountains to this list and squeeze out our spiritual life which is why we must let some of the list go. However, it would be dysfunctional to ignore basic responsibilities. The following list (no more than 5 items) is the simple version of what actually needs to be done today. Anything else accomplished will be a bonus but is intentionally dropped from expectation less it distract us from our spiritual work.

Responsibilities List:

➢ _____

_____

➢ _____

_____

➢ _____

_____

➢ _____

_____

➢ _____

_____

Clean as You Go

- Frustration

- Resentment

- Fear

- Insecurity

- Upset

When a situation triggers upset we must address it immediately every single time in the moment. Use this prayer and use it consistently during the day when you become upset:

"Allow me to see clarity where I see upset. It is no longer about me."

Evening Soul Surgery

worry   stress   fear   insecurity

think too much   alone   upset   frustration

resentment   overwhelm   defensive   exhausted

hate   anxiety   addiction   codependency

inauthentic   dishonesty   disloyalty   apathy

give up   fakeness   depression   judgement

Circle any of the principles above that come to your mind. Write the things in your life based on the words circled that are still holding you hostage (even if it's a repeat from another entry).

_____

_____

_____

_____

_____

_____

_____

Upon completing the list use the following prayer to wipe your mind clean:

"Allow me to let go of what is upsetting me that I may be healed on the deepest level. Remove my difficulties that I may be present and of greater service."

(Initial)

By initialing you acknowledge that you lived one spiritually responsible day. What you did today is enough to change yourself which enough to change the world. Good job ☺

Daily Practice

Date: _____

Morning Intention

Today is the Day.
Today is all I have. Today is all I need.

"Free me from the bondage of self that I may live in the present and with authenticity. Allow me to be the person I am meant to be as a light shining in this world serving others still in need."

playful   creative   meaning   grateful   service
joyful   purpose   passion   inspiration
compassion   contentment   forgiveness
tolerance   loving   acceptance   intuition
integrity   honesty   loyalty   perseverance
authenticity   genuineness

Circle one of the principles above to bring in light for today. In the following lines write the actions or behaviors that you intend to do today to bring these concepts alive in your life. Keep it simple.

_____

_____

_____

_____

_____

_____

_____

_____

Each day we have responsibilities that require our action. It is easy to add mountains to this list and squeeze out our spiritual life which is why we must let some of the list go. However, it would be dysfunctional to ignore basic responsibilities. The following list (no more than 5 items) is the simple version of what actually needs to be done today. Anything else accomplished will be a bonus but is intentionally dropped from expectation less it distract us from our spiritual work.

Responsibilities List:

➢ _____

_____

➢ _____

_____

➢ _____

_____

➢ _____

_____

➢ _____

_____

Clean as You Go

- Frustration
- Resentment
- Fear
- Insecurity
- Upset

When a situation triggers upset we must address it immediately every single time in the moment. Use this prayer and use it consistently during the day when you become upset:

"Allow me to see clarity where I see upset. It is no longer about me."

Evening Soul Surgery

worry   stress   fear   insecurity

think too much   alone   upset   frustration

resentment   overwhelm   defensive   exhausted

hate   anxiety   addiction   codependency

inauthentic   dishonesty   disloyalty   apathy

give up   fakeness   depression   judgement

Circle any of the principles above that come to your mind. Write the things in your life based on the words circled that are still holding you hostage (even if it's a repeat from another entry).

_____

_____

_____

_____

_____

_____

_____

Upon completing the list use the following prayer to wipe your mind clean:

"Allow me to let go of what is upsetting me that I may be healed on the deepest level. Remove my difficulties that I may be present and of greater service."

(Initial)

By initialing you acknowledge that you lived one spiritually responsible day. What you did today is enough to change yourself which enough to change the world. Good job ☺

Daily Practice

Date: _____

Morning Intention

Today is the Day.
Today is all I have. Today is all I need.

"Free me from the bondage of self that I may live in the present and with authenticity. Allow me to be the person I am meant to be as a light shining in this world serving others still in need."

playful   creative   meaning   grateful   service
joyful   purpose   passion   inspiration
compassion   contentment   forgiveness
tolerance   loving   acceptance   intuition
integrity   honesty   loyalty   perseverance
authenticity   genuineness

Circle one of the principles above to bring in light for today. In the following lines write the actions or behaviors that you intend to do today to bring these concepts alive in your life. Keep it simple.

_____

_____

_____

_____

_____

_____

_____

Each day we have responsibilities that require our action. It is easy to add mountains to this list and squeeze out our spiritual life which is why we must let some of the list go. However, it would be dysfunctional to ignore basic responsibilities. The following list (no more than 5 items) is the simple version of what actually needs to be done today. Anything else accomplished will be a bonus but is intentionally dropped from expectation less it distract us from our spiritual work.

Responsibilities List:

➤ _____

_____

➤ _____

_____

➤ _____

_____

➤ _____

_____

➤ _____

_____

Clean as You Go

- Frustration
- Resentment
- Fear
- Insecurity
- Upset

When a situation triggers upset we must address it immediately every single time in the moment. Use this prayer and use it consistently during the day when you become upset:

"Allow me to see clarity where I see upset. It is no longer about me."

Evening Soul Surgery

worry   stress   fear   insecurity

think too much   alone   upset   frustration

resentment   overwhelm   defensive   exhausted

hate   anxiety   addiction   codependency

inauthentic   dishonesty   disloyalty   apathy

give up   fakeness   depression   judgement

Circle any of the principles above that come to your mind. Write the things in your life based on the words circled that are still holding you hostage (even if it's a repeat from another entry).

_____

_____

_____

_____

_____

_____

_____

_____

Upon completing the list use the following prayer to wipe your mind clean:

"Allow me to let go of what is upsetting me that I may be healed on the deepest level. Remove my difficulties that I may be present and of greater service."

_____

(Initial)

By initialing you acknowledge that you lived one spiritually responsible day. What you did today is enough to change yourself which enough to change the world. Good job ☺

Daily Practice

Date: _____

Morning Intention

Today is the Day.
Today is all I have. Today is all I need.

"Free me from the bondage of self that I may live in the present and with authenticity. Allow me to be the person I am meant to be as a light shining in this world serving others still in need."

playful   creative   meaning   grateful   service
joyful   purpose   passion   inspiration
compassion   contentment   forgiveness
tolerance   loving   acceptance   intuition
integrity   honesty   loyalty   perseverance
authenticity   genuineness

Circle one of the principles above to bring in light for today. In the following lines write the actions or behaviors that you intend to do today to bring these concepts alive in your life. Keep it simple.

_____

_____

_____

_____

_____

_____

_____

_____

Each day we have responsibilities that require our action. It is easy to add mountains to this list and squeeze out our spiritual life which is why we must let some of the list go. However, it would be dysfunctional to ignore basic responsibilities. The following list (no more than 5 items) is the simple version of what actually needs to be done today. Anything else accomplished will be a bonus but is intentionally dropped from expectation less it distract us from our spiritual work.

Responsibilities List:

➤ _____

_____

➤ _____

_____

➤ _____

_____

➤ _____

_____

➤ _____

_____

Clean as You Go

- Frustration
- Resentment
- Fear
- Insecurity
- Upset

When a situation triggers upset we must address it immediately every single time in the moment. Use this prayer and use it consistently during the day when you become upset:

"Allow me to see clarity where I see upset. It is no longer about me."

Evening Soul Surgery

worry   stress   fear   insecurity

think too much   alone   upset   frustration

resentment   overwhelm   defensive   exhausted

hate   anxiety   addiction   codependency

inauthentic   dishonesty   disloyalty   apathy

give up   fakeness   depression   judgement

Circle any of the principles above that come to your mind. Write the things in your life based on the words circled that are still holding you hostage (even if it's a repeat from another entry).

_____

_____

_____

_____

_____

_____

_____

_____

Upon completing the list use the following prayer to wipe your mind clean:

"Allow me to let go of what is upsetting me that I may be healed on the deepest level. Remove my difficulties that I may be present and of greater service."

(Initial)

By initialing you acknowledge that you lived one spiritually responsible day. What you did today is enough to change yourself which enough to change the world. Good job ☺

Daily Practice

Date: _____

Morning Intention

Today is the Day.
Today is all I have. Today is all I need.

"Free me from the bondage of self that I may live in the present and with authenticity. Allow me to be the person I am meant to be as a light shining in this world serving others still in need."

playful   creative   meaning   grateful   service

joyful   purpose   passion   inspiration

compassion   contentment   forgiveness

tolerance   loving   acceptance   intuition

integrity   honesty   loyalty   perseverance

authenticity   genuineness

Circle one of the principles above to bring in light for today. In the following lines write the actions or behaviors that you intend to do today to bring these concepts alive in your life. Keep it simple.

_____

_____

_____

_____

_____

_____

_____

Each day we have responsibilities that require our action. It is easy to add mountains to this list and squeeze out our spiritual life which is why we must let some of the list go. However, it would be dysfunctional to ignore basic responsibilities. The following list (no more than 5 items) is the simple version of what actually needs to be done today. Anything else accomplished will be a bonus but is intentionally dropped from expectation less it distract us from our spiritual work.

Responsibilities List:

➤ _____

_____

➤ _____

_____

➤ _____

_____

➤ _____

_____

➤ _____

_____

Clean as You Go

- Frustration
- Resentment
- Fear
- Insecurity
- Upset

When a situation triggers upset we must address it immediately every single time in the moment. Use this prayer and use it consistently during the day when you become upset:

"Allow me to see clarity where I see upset. It is no longer about me."

Evening Soul Surgery

worry   stress   fear   insecurity

think too much   alone   upset   frustration

resentment   overwhelm   defensive   exhausted

hate   anxiety   addiction   codependency

inauthentic   dishonesty   disloyalty   apathy

give up   fakeness   depression   judgement

Circle any of the principles above that come to your mind. Write the things in your life based on the words circled that are still holding you hostage (even if it's a repeat from another entry).

_____

_____

_____

_____

_____

_____

_____

_____

Upon completing the list use the following prayer to wipe your mind clean:

"Allow me to let go of what is upsetting me that I may be healed on the deepest level. Remove my difficulties that I may be present and of greater service."

———————

(Initial)

By initialing you acknowledge that you lived one spiritually responsible day. What you did today is enough to change yourself which enough to change the world. Good job ☺

Daily Practice

Date: _____

Morning Intention

Today is the Day.
Today is all I have. Today is all I need.

"Free me from the bondage of self that I may live in the present and with authenticity. Allow me to be the person I am meant to be as a light shining in this world serving others still in need."

playful   creative   meaning   grateful   service

joyful   purpose   passion   inspiration

compassion   contentment   forgiveness

tolerance   loving   acceptance   intuition

integrity   honesty   loyalty   perseverance

authenticity   genuineness

Circle one of the principles above to bring in light for today. In the following lines write the actions or behaviors that you intend to do today to bring these concepts alive in your life. Keep it simple.

_____

_____

_____

_____

_____

_____

_____

Each day we have responsibilities that require our action. It is easy to add mountains to this list and squeeze out our spiritual life which is why we must let some of the list go. However, it would be dysfunctional to ignore basic responsibilities. The following list (no more than 5 items) is the simple version of what actually needs to be done today. Anything else accomplished will be a bonus but is intentionally dropped from expectation less it distract us from our spiritual work.

Responsibilities List:

➤ _____

_____

➤ _____

_____

➤ _____

_____

➤ _____

_____

➤ _____

_____

Clean as You Go

- Frustration

- Resentment

- Fear

- Insecurity

- Upset

When a situation triggers upset we must address it immediately every single time in the moment. Use this prayer and use it consistently during the day when you become upset:

"Allow me to see clarity where I see upset. It is no longer about me."

Evening Soul Surgery

worry   stress   fear   insecurity

think too much   alone   upset   frustration

resentment   overwhelm   defensive   exhausted

hate   anxiety   addiction   codependency

inauthentic   dishonesty   disloyalty   apathy

give up   fakeness   depression   judgement

Circle any of the principles above that come to your mind. Write the things in your life based on the words circled that are still holding you hostage (even if it's a repeat from another entry).

_____

_____

_____

_____

_____

_____

_____

Upon completing the list use the following prayer to wipe your mind clean:

"Allow me to let go of what is upsetting me that I may be healed on the deepest level. Remove my difficulties that I may be present and of greater service."

(Initial)

By initialing you acknowledge that you lived one spiritually responsible day. What you did today is enough to change yourself which enough to change the world. Good job ☺

Daily Practice

Date: _____

Morning Intention

Today is the Day.
Today is all I have. Today is all I need.

"Free me from the bondage of self that I
may live in the present and with
authenticity. Allow me to be the person I
am meant to be as a light shining in this
world serving others still in need."

playful   creative   meaning   grateful   service
joyful   purpose   passion   inspiration
compassion   contentment   forgiveness
tolerance   loving   acceptance   intuition
integrity   honesty   loyalty   perseverance
authenticity   genuineness

Circle one of the principles above to bring in light for today. In the following lines write the actions or behaviors that you intend to do today to bring these concepts alive in your life. Keep it simple.

_____

_____

_____

_____

_____

_____

_____

_____

Each day we have responsibilities that require our action. It is easy to add mountains to this list and squeeze out our spiritual life which is why we must let some of the list go. However, it would be dysfunctional to ignore basic responsibilities. The following list (no more than 5 items) is the simple version of what actually needs to be done today. Anything else accomplished will be a bonus but is intentionally dropped from expectation less it distract us from our spiritual work.

Responsibilities List:

➤ _____

_____

➤ _____

_____

➤ _____

_____

➤ _____

_____

➤ _____

_____

Clean as You Go

- Frustration
- Resentment
- Fear
- Insecurity
- Upset

When a situation triggers upset we must address it immediately every single time in the moment. Use this prayer and use it consistently during the day when you become upset:

"Allow me to see clarity where I see upset. It is no longer about me."

Evening Soul Surgery

worry   stress   fear   insecurity

think too much   alone   upset   frustration

resentment   overwhelm   defensive   exhausted

hate   anxiety   addiction   codependency

inauthentic   dishonesty   disloyalty   apathy

give up   fakeness   depression   judgement

Circle any of the principles above that come to your mind. Write the things in your life based on the words circled that are still holding you hostage (even if it's a repeat from another entry).

_____

_____

_____

_____

_____

_____

_____

Upon completing the list use the following prayer to wipe your mind clean:

"Allow me to let go of what is upsetting me that I may be healed on the deepest level. Remove my difficulties that I may be present and of greater service."

(Initial)

By initialing you acknowledge that you lived one spiritually responsible day. What you did today is enough to change yourself which enough to change the world. Good job ☺

Daily Practice

Date: _____

Morning Intention

Today is the Day.
Today is all I have. Today is all I need.

"Free me from the bondage of self that I may live in the present and with authenticity. Allow me to be the person I am meant to be as a light shining in this world serving others still in need."

playful   creative   meaning   grateful   service

joyful   purpose   passion   inspiration

compassion   contentment   forgiveness

tolerance   loving   acceptance   intuition

integrity   honesty   loyalty   perseverance

authenticity   genuineness

Circle one of the principles above to bring in light for today. In the following lines write the actions or behaviors that you intend to do today to bring these concepts alive in your life. Keep it simple.

_____

_____

_____

_____

_____

_____

_____

Each day we have responsibilities that require our action. It is easy to add mountains to this list and squeeze out our spiritual life which is why we must let some of the list go. However, it would be dysfunctional to ignore basic responsibilities. The following list (no more than 5 items) is the simple version of what actually needs to be done today. Anything else accomplished will be a bonus but is intentionally dropped from expectation less it distract us from our spiritual work.

Responsibilities List:

➢ _____

_____

➢ _____

_____

➢ _____

_____

➢ _____

_____

➢ _____

_____

Clean as You Go

- Frustration
- Resentment
- Fear
- Insecurity
- Upset

When a situation triggers upset we must address it immediately every single time in the moment. Use this prayer and use it consistently during the day when you become upset:

"Allow me to see clarity where I see upset. It is no longer about me."

Evening Soul Surgery

worry   stress   fear   insecurity

think too much   alone   upset   frustration

resentment   overwhelm   defensive   exhausted

hate   anxiety   addiction   codependency

inauthentic   dishonesty   disloyalty   apathy

give up   fakeness   depression   judgement

Circle any of the principles above that come to your mind. Write the things in your life based on the words circled that are still holding you hostage (even if it's a repeat from another entry).

_____

_____

_____

_____

_____

_____

_____

Upon completing the list use the following prayer to wipe your mind clean:

"Allow me to let go of what is upsetting me that I may be healed on the deepest level. Remove my difficulties that I may be present and of greater service."

_____

(Initial)

By initialing you acknowledge that you lived one spiritually responsible day. What you did today is enough to change yourself which enough to change the world. Good job ☺

Daily Practice

Date: _____

Morning Intention

Today is the Day.
Today is all I have. Today is all I need.

"Free me from the bondage of self that I may live in the present and with authenticity. Allow me to be the person I am meant to be as a light shining in this world serving others still in need."

playful   creative   meaning   grateful   service

joyful   purpose   passion   inspiration

compassion   contentment   forgiveness

tolerance   loving   acceptance   intuition

integrity   honesty   loyalty   perseverance

authenticity   genuineness

Circle one of the principles above to bring in light for today. In the following lines write the actions or behaviors that you intend to do today to bring these concepts alive in your life. Keep it simple.

_____

_____

_____

_____

_____

_____

_____

Each day we have responsibilities that require our action. It is easy to add mountains to this list and squeeze out our spiritual life which is why we must let some of the list go. However, it would be dysfunctional to ignore basic responsibilities. The following list (no more than 5 items) is the simple version of what actually needs to be done today. Anything else accomplished will be a bonus but is intentionally dropped from expectation less it distract us from our spiritual work.

Responsibilities List:

➢ _____

_____

➢ _____

_____

➢ _____

_____

➢ _____

_____

➢ _____

_____

Clean as You Go

- Frustration

- Resentment

- Fear

- Insecurity

- Upset

When a situation triggers upset we must address it immediately every single time in the moment. Use this prayer and use it consistently during the day when you become upset:

"Allow me to see clarity where I see upset. It is no longer about me."

Evening Soul Surgery

worry   stress   fear   insecurity

think too much   alone   upset   frustration

resentment   overwhelm   defensive   exhausted

hate   anxiety   addiction   codependency

inauthentic   dishonesty   disloyalty   apathy

give up   fakeness   depression   judgement

Circle any of the principles above that come to your mind. Write the things in your life based on the words circled that are still holding you hostage (even if it's a repeat from another entry).

_____

_____

_____

_____

_____

_____

_____

Upon completing the list use the following prayer to wipe your mind clean:

"Allow me to let go of what is upsetting me that I may be healed on the deepest level. Remove my difficulties that I may be present and of greater service."

_____

(Initial)

By initialing you acknowledge that you lived one spiritually responsible day. What you did today is enough to change yourself which enough to change the world. Good job ☺

Daily Practice

Date: _____

Morning Intention

Today is the Day.
Today is all I have. Today is all I need.

"Free me from the bondage of self that I may live in the present and with authenticity. Allow me to be the person I am meant to be as a light shining in this world serving others still in need."

playful   creative   meaning   grateful   service

joyful   purpose   passion   inspiration

compassion   contentment   forgiveness

tolerance   loving   acceptance   intuition

integrity   honesty   loyalty   perseverance

authenticity   genuineness

Circle one of the principles above to bring in light for today. In the following lines write the actions or behaviors that you intend to do today to bring these concepts alive in your life. Keep it simple.

_____

_____

_____

_____

_____

_____

_____

Each day we have responsibilities that require our action. It is easy to add mountains to this list and squeeze out our spiritual life which is why we must let some of the list go. However, it would be dysfunctional to ignore basic responsibilities. The following list (no more than 5 items) is the simple version of what actually needs to be done today. Anything else accomplished will be a bonus but is intentionally dropped from expectation less it distract us from our spiritual work.

Responsibilities List:

➢ _____

_____

➢ _____

_____

➢ _____

_____

➢ _____

_____

➢ _____

_____

Clean as You Go

- Frustration

- Resentment

- Fear

- Insecurity

- Upset

When a situation triggers upset we must address it immediately every single time in the moment. Use this prayer and use it consistently during the day when you become upset:

"Allow me to see clarity where I see upset. It is no longer about me."

Evening Soul Surgery

worry   stress   fear   insecurity

think too much   alone   upset   frustration

resentment   overwhelm   defensive   exhausted

hate   anxiety   addiction   codependency

inauthentic   dishonesty   disloyalty   apathy

give up   fakeness   depression   judgement

Circle any of the principles above that come to your mind. Write the things in your life based on the words circled that are still holding you hostage (even if it's a repeat from another entry).

_____

_____

_____

_____

_____

_____

_____

Upon completing the list use the following prayer to wipe your mind clean:

"Allow me to let go of what is upsetting me that I may be healed on the deepest level. Remove my difficulties that I may be present and of greater service."

_____

(*Initial*)

By initialing you acknowledge that you lived one spiritually responsible day. What you did today is enough to change yourself which enough to change the world. Good job ☺

Daily Practice

Date: _____

<u>Morning Intention</u>

Today is the Day.
Today is all I have. Today is all I need.

"Free me from the bondage of self that I may live in the present and with authenticity. Allow me to be the person I am meant to be as a light shining in this world serving others still in need."

playful   creative   meaning   grateful   service

joyful   purpose   passion   inspiration

compassion   contentment   forgiveness

tolerance   loving   acceptance   intuition

integrity   honesty   loyalty   perseverance

authenticity   genuineness

Circle one of the principles above to bring in light for today. In the following lines write the actions or behaviors that you intend to do today to bring these concepts alive in your life. Keep it simple.

_____

_____

_____

_____

_____

_____

_____

Each day we have responsibilities that require our action. It is easy to add mountains to this list and squeeze out our spiritual life which is why we must let some of the list go. However, it would be dysfunctional to ignore basic responsibilities. The following list (no more than 5 items) is the simple version of what actually needs to be done today. Anything else accomplished will be a bonus but is intentionally dropped from expectation less it distract us from our spiritual work.

Responsibilities List:

➢ _____

_____

➢ _____

_____

➢ _____

_____

➢ _____

_____

➢ _____

_____

Clean as You Go

- Frustration
- Resentment
- Fear
- Insecurity
- Upset

When a situation triggers upset we must address it immediately every single time in the moment. Use this prayer and use it consistently during the day when you become upset:

"Allow me to see clarity where I see upset. It is no longer about me."

Evening Soul Surgery

worry   stress   fear   insecurity

think too much   alone   upset   frustration

resentment   overwhelm   defensive   exhausted

hate   anxiety   addiction   codependency

inauthentic   dishonesty   disloyalty   apathy

give up   fakeness   depression   judgement

Circle any of the principles above that come to your mind. Write the things in your life based on the words circled that are still holding you hostage (even if it's a repeat from another entry).

_____

_____

_____

_____

_____

_____

_____

Upon completing the list use the following prayer to wipe your mind clean:

"Allow me to let go of what is upsetting me that I may be healed on the deepest level. Remove my difficulties that I may be present and of greater service."

(Initial)

By initialing you acknowledge that you lived one spiritually responsible day. What you did today is enough to change yourself which enough to change the world. Good job ☺

Daily Practice

Date: _____

Morning Intention

Today is the Day.
Today is all I have. Today is all I need.

"Free me from the bondage of self that I may live in the present and with authenticity. Allow me to be the person I am meant to be as a light shining in this world serving others still in need."

playful   creative   meaning   grateful   service

joyful   purpose   passion   inspiration

compassion   contentment   forgiveness

tolerance   loving   acceptance   intuition

integrity   honesty   loyalty   perseverance

authenticity   genuineness

Circle one of the principles above to bring in light for today. In the following lines write the actions or behaviors that you intend to do today to bring these concepts alive in your life. Keep it simple.

_____

_____

_____

_____

_____

_____

_____

Each day we have responsibilities that require our action. It is easy to add mountains to this list and squeeze out our spiritual life which is why we must let some of the list go. However, it would be dysfunctional to ignore basic responsibilities. The following list (no more than 5 items) is the simple version of what actually needs to be done today. Anything else accomplished will be a bonus but is intentionally dropped from expectation less it distract us from our spiritual work.

Responsibilities List:

➢ _____

_____

➢ _____

_____

➢ _____

_____

➢ _____

_____

➢ _____

_____

Clean as You Go

- Frustration
- Resentment
- Fear
- Insecurity
- Upset

When a situation triggers upset we must address it immediately every single time in the moment. Use this prayer and use it consistently during the day when you become upset:

"Allow me to see clarity where I see upset. It is no longer about me."

Evening Soul Surgery

worry   stress   fear   insecurity

think too much   alone   upset   frustration

resentment   overwhelm   defensive   exhausted

hate   anxiety   addiction   codependency

inauthentic   dishonesty   disloyalty   apathy

give up   fakeness   depression   judgement

Circle any of the principles above that come to your mind. Write the things in your life based on the words circled that are still holding you hostage (even if it's a repeat from another entry).

_____

_____

_____

_____

_____

_____

_____

Upon completing the list use the following prayer to wipe your mind clean:

"Allow me to let go of what is upsetting me that I may be healed on the deepest level. Remove my difficulties that I may be present and of greater service."

_____

(Initial)

By initialing you acknowledge that you lived one spiritually responsible day. What you did today is enough to change yourself which enough to change the world. Good job ☺

Daily Practice

Date: _____

<u>Morning Intention</u>

Today is the Day.
Today is all I have. Today is all I need.

"Free me from the bondage of self that I may live in the present and with authenticity. Allow me to be the person I am meant to be as a light shining in this world serving others still in need."

playful   creative   meaning   grateful   service
joyful   purpose   passion   inspiration
compassion   contentment   forgiveness
tolerance   loving   acceptance   intuition
integrity   honesty   loyalty   perseverance
authenticity   genuineness

Circle one of the principles above to bring in light for today. In the following lines write the actions or behaviors that you intend to do today to bring these concepts alive in your life. Keep it simple.

_____

_____

_____

_____

_____

_____

_____

Each day we have responsibilities that require our action. It is easy to add mountains to this list and squeeze out our spiritual life which is why we must let some of the list go. However, it would be dysfunctional to ignore basic responsibilities. The following list (no more than 5 items) is the simple version of what actually needs to be done today. Anything else accomplished will be a bonus but is intentionally dropped from expectation less it distract us from our spiritual work.

Responsibilities List:

➤ _____

_____

➤ _____

_____

➤ _____

_____

➤ _____

_____

➤ _____

_____

Clean as You Go

- Frustration
- Resentment
- Fear
- Insecurity
- Upset

When a situation triggers upset we must address it immediately every single time in the moment. Use this prayer and use it consistently during the day when you become upset:

"Allow me to see clarity where I see upset. It is no longer about me."

Evening Soul Surgery

worry   stress   fear   insecurity

think too much   alone   upset   frustration

resentment   overwhelm   defensive   exhausted

hate   anxiety   addiction   codependency

inauthentic   dishonesty   disloyalty   apathy

give up   fakeness   depression   judgement

Circle any of the principles above that come to your mind. Write the things in your life based on the words circled that are still holding you hostage (even if it's a repeat from another entry).

_____

_____

_____

_____

_____

_____

_____

Upon completing the list use the following prayer to wipe your mind clean:

"Allow me to let go of what is upsetting me that I may be healed on the deepest level. Remove my difficulties that I may be present and of greater service."

—————

(Initial)

By initialing you acknowledge that you lived one spiritually responsible day. What you did today is enough to change yourself which enough to change the world. Good job ☺

Daily Practice

Date: _____

<u>Morning Intention</u>

Today is the Day.
Today is all I have. Today is all I need.

"Free me from the bondage of self that I
may live in the present and with
authenticity. Allow me to be the person I
am meant to be as a light shining in this
world serving others still in need."

playful   creative   meaning   grateful   service
joyful   purpose   passion   inspiration
compassion   contentment   forgiveness
tolerance   loving   acceptance   intuition
integrity   honesty   loyalty   perseverance
authenticity   genuineness

Circle one of the principles above to bring in light for today. In the following lines write the actions or behaviors that you intend to do today to bring these concepts alive in your life. Keep it simple.

_____

_____

_____

_____

_____

_____

_____

_____

Each day we have responsibilities that require our action. It is easy to add mountains to this list and squeeze out our spiritual life which is why we must let some of the list go. However, it would be dysfunctional to ignore basic responsibilities. The following list (no more than 5 items) is the simple version of what actually needs to be done today. Anything else accomplished will be a bonus but is intentionally dropped from expectation less it distract us from our spiritual work.

Responsibilities List:

➢ _____

_____

➢ _____

_____

➢ _____

_____

➢ _____

_____

➢ _____

_____

Clean as You Go

- Frustration
- Resentment
- Fear
- Insecurity
- Upset

When a situation triggers upset we must address it immediately every single time in the moment. Use this prayer and use it consistently during the day when you become upset:

"Allow me to see clarity where I see upset. It is no longer about me."

Evening Soul Surgery

worry   stress   fear   insecurity

think too much   alone   upset   frustration

resentment   overwhelm   defensive   exhausted

hate   anxiety   addiction   codependency

inauthentic   dishonesty   disloyalty   apathy

give up   fakeness   depression   judgement

Circle any of the principles above that come to your mind. Write the things in your life based on the words circled that are still holding you hostage (even if it's a repeat from another entry).

_____

_____

_____

_____

_____

_____

_____

Upon completing the list use the following prayer to wipe your mind clean:

"Allow me to let go of what is upsetting me that I may be healed on the deepest level. Remove my difficulties that I may be present and of greater service."

_____

(Initial)

By initialing you acknowledge that you lived one spiritually responsible day. What you did today is enough to change yourself which enough to change the world. Good job ☺

Daily Practice

Date: _____

<u>Morning Intention</u>

Today is the Day.
Today is all I have. Today is all I need.

"Free me from the bondage of self that I may live in the present and with authenticity. Allow me to be the person I am meant to be as a light shining in this world serving others still in need."

playful   creative   meaning   grateful   service

joyful   purpose   passion   inspiration

compassion   contentment   forgiveness

tolerance   loving   acceptance   intuition

integrity   honesty   loyalty   perseverance

authenticity   genuineness

Circle one of the principles above to bring in light for today. In the following lines write the actions or behaviors that you intend to do today to bring these concepts alive in your life. Keep it simple.

_____

_____

_____

_____

_____

_____

_____

Each day we have responsibilities that require our action. It is easy to add mountains to this list and squeeze out our spiritual life which is why we must let some of the list go. However, it would be dysfunctional to ignore basic responsibilities. The following list (no more than 5 items) is the simple version of what actually needs to be done today. Anything else accomplished will be a bonus but is intentionally dropped from expectation less it distract us from our spiritual work.

Responsibilities List:

➤ _____

_____

➤ _____

_____

➤ _____

_____

➤ _____

_____

➤ _____

_____

Clean as You Go

- Frustration

- Resentment

- Fear

- Insecurity

- Upset

When a situation triggers upset we must address it immediately every single time in the moment. Use this prayer and use it consistently during the day when you become upset:

"Allow me to see clarity where I see upset. It is no longer about me."

Evening Soul Surgery

worry   stress   fear   insecurity

think too much   alone   upset   frustration

resentment   overwhelm   defensive   exhausted

hate   anxiety   addiction   codependency

inauthentic   dishonesty   disloyalty   apathy

give up   fakeness   depression   judgement

Circle any of the principles above that come to your mind. Write the things in your life based on the words circled that are still holding you hostage (even if it's a repeat from another entry).

_____

_____

_____

_____

_____

_____

_____

Upon completing the list use the following prayer to wipe your mind clean:

"Allow me to let go of what is upsetting me that I may be healed on the deepest level. Remove my difficulties that I may be present and of greater service."

———————————

(Initial)

By initialing you acknowledge that you lived one spiritually responsible day. What you did today is enough to change yourself which enough to change the world. Good job ☺

Daily Practice

Date: _____

Morning Intention

Today is the Day.
Today is all I have. Today is all I need.

"Free me from the bondage of self that I may live in the present and with authenticity. Allow me to be the person I am meant to be as a light shining in this world serving others still in need."

playful   creative   meaning   grateful   service
joyful   purpose   passion   inspiration
compassion   contentment   forgiveness
tolerance   loving   acceptance   intuition
integrity   honesty   loyalty   perseverance
authenticity   genuineness

Circle one of the principles above to bring in light for today. In the following lines write the actions or behaviors that you intend to do today to bring these concepts alive in your life. Keep it simple.

_____

_____

_____

_____

_____

_____

_____

_____

Each day we have responsibilities that require our action. It is easy to add mountains to this list and squeeze out our spiritual life which is why we must let some of the list go. However, it would be dysfunctional to ignore basic responsibilities. The following list (no more than 5 items) is the simple version of what actually needs to be done today. Anything else accomplished will be a bonus but is intentionally dropped from expectation less it distract us from our spiritual work.

Responsibilities List:

➢ _____

_____

➢ _____

_____

➢ _____

_____

➢ _____

_____

➢ _____

_____

Clean as You Go

- Frustration

- Resentment

- Fear

- Insecurity

- Upset

When a situation triggers upset we must address it immediately every single time in the moment. Use this prayer and use it consistently during the day when you become upset:

"Allow me to see clarity where I see upset. It is no longer about me."

Evening Soul Surgery

worry   stress   fear   insecurity

think too much   alone   upset   frustration

resentment   overwhelm   defensive   exhausted

hate   anxiety   addiction   codependency

inauthentic   dishonesty   disloyalty   apathy

give up   fakeness   depression   judgement

Circle any of the principles above that come to your mind. Write the things in your life based on the words circled that are still holding you hostage (even if it's a repeat from another entry).

_____

_____

_____

_____

_____

_____

_____

Upon completing the list use the following prayer to wipe your mind clean:

"Allow me to let go of what is upsetting me that I may be healed on the deepest level. Remove my difficulties that I may be present and of greater service."

_____

(Initial)

By initialing you acknowledge that you lived one spiritually responsible day. What you did today is enough to change yourself which enough to change the world. Good job ☺

Daily Practice

Date: _____

Morning Intention

Today is the Day.
Today is all I have. Today is all I need.

"Free me from the bondage of self that I may live in the present and with authenticity. Allow me to be the person I am meant to be as a light shining in this world serving others still in need."

playful   creative   meaning   grateful   service

joyful   purpose   passion   inspiration

compassion   contentment   forgiveness

tolerance   loving   acceptance   intuition

integrity   honesty   loyalty   perseverance

authenticity   genuineness

Circle one of the principles above to bring in light for today. In the following lines write the actions or behaviors that you intend to do today to bring these concepts alive in your life. Keep it simple.

_____

_____

_____

_____

_____

_____

_____

Each day we have responsibilities that require our action. It is easy to add mountains to this list and squeeze out our spiritual life which is why we must let some of the list go. However, it would be dysfunctional to ignore basic responsibilities. The following list (no more than 5 items) is the simple version of what actually needs to be done today. Anything else accomplished will be a bonus but is intentionally dropped from expectation less it distract us from our spiritual work.

Responsibilities List:

➤ _____

_____

➤ _____

_____

➤ _____

_____

➤ _____

_____

➤ _____

_____

Clean as You Go

- Frustration
- Resentment
- Fear
- Insecurity
- Upset

When a situation triggers upset we must address it immediately every single time in the moment. Use this prayer and use it consistently during the day when you become upset:

"Allow me to see clarity where I see upset. It is no longer about me."

Evening Soul Surgery

worry   stress   fear   insecurity

think too much   alone   upset   frustration

resentment   overwhelm   defensive   exhausted

hate   anxiety   addiction   codependency

inauthentic   dishonesty   disloyalty   apathy

give up   fakeness   depression   judgement

Circle any of the principles above that come to your mind. Write the things in your life based on the words circled that are still holding you hostage (even if it's a repeat from another entry).

_____

_____

_____

_____

_____

_____

_____

Upon completing the list use the following prayer to wipe your mind clean:

"Allow me to let go of what is upsetting me that I may be healed on the deepest level. Remove my difficulties that I may be present and of greater service."

(Initial)

By initialing you acknowledge that you lived one spiritually responsible day. What you did today is enough to change yourself which enough to change the world. Good job ☺

Daily Practice

Date: _____

Morning Intention

Today is the Day.
Today is all I have. Today is all I need.

"Free me from the bondage of self that I
may live in the present and with
authenticity. Allow me to be the person I
am meant to be as a light shining in this
world serving others still in need."

playful   creative   meaning   grateful   service

joyful   purpose   passion   inspiration

compassion   contentment   forgiveness

tolerance   loving   acceptance   intuition

integrity   honesty   loyalty   perseverance

authenticity   genuineness

Circle one of the principles above to bring in light for today. In the following lines write the actions or behaviors that you intend to do today to bring these concepts alive in your life. Keep it simple.

_____

_____

_____

_____

_____

_____

_____

Each day we have responsibilities that require our action. It is easy to add mountains to this list and squeeze out our spiritual life which is why we must let some of the list go. However, it would be dysfunctional to ignore basic responsibilities. The following list (no more than 5 items) is the simple version of what actually needs to be done today. Anything else accomplished will be a bonus but is intentionally dropped from expectation less it distract us from our spiritual work.

Responsibilities List:

➤ _____

_____

➤ _____

_____

➤ _____

_____

➤ _____

_____

➤ _____

_____

Clean as You Go

- Frustration
- Resentment
- Fear
- Insecurity
- Upset

When a situation triggers upset we must address it immediately every single time in the moment. Use this prayer and use it consistently during the day when you become upset:

"Allow me to see clarity where I see upset. It is no longer about me."

Evening Soul Surgery

worry   stress   fear   insecurity

think too much   alone   upset   frustration

resentment   overwhelm   defensive   exhausted

hate   anxiety   addiction   codependency

inauthentic   dishonesty   disloyalty   apathy

give up   fakeness   depression   judgement

Circle any of the principles above that come to your mind. Write the things in your life based on the words circled that are still holding you hostage (even if it's a repeat from another entry).

_____

_____

_____

_____

_____

_____

_____

Upon completing the list use the following prayer to wipe your mind clean:

"Allow me to let go of what is upsetting me that I may be healed on the deepest level. Remove my difficulties that I may be present and of greater service."

(Initial)

By initialing you acknowledge that you lived one spiritually responsible day. What you did today is enough to change yourself which enough to change the world. Good job ☺

Daily Practice

Date: _____

Morning Intention

Today is the Day.
Today is all I have. Today is all I need.

"Free me from the bondage of self that I may live in the present and with authenticity. Allow me to be the person I am meant to be as a light shining in this world serving others still in need."

playful   creative   meaning   grateful   service
joyful   purpose   passion   inspiration
compassion   contentment   forgiveness
tolerance   loving   acceptance   intuition
integrity   honesty   loyalty   perseverance
authenticity   genuineness

Circle one of the principles above to bring in light for today. In the following lines write the actions or behaviors that you intend to do today to bring these concepts alive in your life. Keep it simple.

_____

_____

_____

_____

_____

_____

_____

Each day we have responsibilities that require our action. It is easy to add mountains to this list and squeeze out our spiritual life which is why we must let some of the list go. However, it would be dysfunctional to ignore basic responsibilities. The following list (no more than 5 items) is the simple version of what actually needs to be done today. Anything else accomplished will be a bonus but is intentionally dropped from expectation less it distract us from our spiritual work.

Responsibilities List:

➢ _____

_____

➢ _____

_____

➢ _____

_____

➢ _____

_____

➢ _____

_____

Clean as You Go

- Frustration
- Resentment
- Fear
- Insecurity
- Upset

When a situation triggers upset we must address it immediately every single time in the moment. Use this prayer and use it consistently during the day when you become upset:

"Allow me to see clarity where I see upset. It is no longer about me."

Evening Soul Surgery

worry   stress   fear   insecurity

think too much   alone   upset   frustration

resentment   overwhelm   defensive   exhausted

hate   anxiety   addiction   codependency

inauthentic   dishonesty   disloyalty   apathy

give up   fakeness   depression   judgement

Circle any of the principles above that come to your
mind. Write the things in your life based on the words
circled that are still holding you hostage (even if it's a
repeat from another entry).

_____

_____

_____

_____

_____

_____

_____

Upon completing the list use the following prayer to wipe your mind clean:

"Allow me to let go of what is upsetting me that I may be healed on the deepest level. Remove my difficulties that I may be present and of greater service."

(Initial)

By initialing you acknowledge that you lived one spiritually responsible day. What you did today is enough to change yourself which enough to change the world. Good job ☺

Daily Practice

Date: _____

Morning Intention

Today is the Day.
Today is all I have. Today is all I need.

"Free me from the bondage of self that I may live in the present and with authenticity. Allow me to be the person I am meant to be as a light shining in this world serving others still in need."

playful   creative   meaning   grateful   service
joyful   purpose   passion   inspiration
compassion   contentment   forgiveness
tolerance   loving   acceptance   intuition
integrity   honesty   loyalty   perseverance
authenticity   genuineness

Circle one of the principles above to bring in light for today. In the following lines write the actions or behaviors that you intend to do today to bring these concepts alive in your life. Keep it simple.

_____

_____

_____

_____

_____

_____

_____

Each day we have responsibilities that require our action. It is easy to add mountains to this list and squeeze out our spiritual life which is why we must let some of the list go. However, it would be dysfunctional to ignore basic responsibilities. The following list (no more than 5 items) is the simple version of what actually needs to be done today. Anything else accomplished will be a bonus but is intentionally dropped from expectation less it distract us from our spiritual work.

Responsibilities List:

➤ _____

_____

➤ _____

_____

➤ _____

_____

➤ _____

_____

➤ _____

_____

Clean as You Go

- Frustration
- Resentment
- Fear
- Insecurity
- Upset

When a situation triggers upset we must address it immediately every single time in the moment. Use this prayer and use it consistently during the day when you become upset:

"Allow me to see clarity where I see upset. It is no longer about me."

Evening Soul Surgery

worry   stress   fear   insecurity

think too much   alone   upset   frustration

resentment   overwhelm   defensive   exhausted

hate   anxiety   addiction   codependency

inauthentic   dishonesty   disloyalty   apathy

give up   fakeness   depression   judgement

Circle any of the principles above that come to your mind. Write the things in your life based on the words circled that are still holding you hostage (even if it's a repeat from another entry).

_____

_____

_____

_____

_____

_____

_____

Upon completing the list use the following prayer to wipe your mind clean:

"Allow me to let go of what is upsetting me that I may be healed on the deepest level. Remove my difficulties that I may be present and of greater service."

_____

(Initial)

By initialing you acknowledge that you lived one spiritually responsible day. What you did today is enough to change yourself which enough to change the world. Good job ☺

Daily Practice

Date: _____

Morning Intention

Today is the Day.
Today is all I have. Today is all I need.

"Free me from the bondage of self that I
may live in the present and with
authenticity. Allow me to be the person I
am meant to be as a light shining in this
world serving others still in need."

playful   creative   meaning   grateful   service

joyful   purpose   passion   inspiration

compassion   contentment   forgiveness

tolerance   loving   acceptance   intuition

integrity   honesty   loyalty   perseverance

authenticity   genuineness

Circle one of the principles above to bring in light for today. In the following lines write the actions or behaviors that you intend to do today to bring these concepts alive in your life. Keep it simple.

_____

_____

_____

_____

_____

_____

_____

Each day we have responsibilities that require our action. It is easy to add mountains to this list and squeeze out our spiritual life which is why we must let some of the list go. However, it would be dysfunctional to ignore basic responsibilities. The following list (no more than 5 items) is the simple version of what actually needs to be done today. Anything else accomplished will be a bonus but is intentionally dropped from expectation less it distract us from our spiritual work.

Responsibilities List:

➢ _____

_____

➢ _____

_____

➢ _____

_____

➢ _____

_____

➢ _____

_____

Clean as You Go

- Frustration
- Resentment
- Fear
- Insecurity
- Upset

When a situation triggers upset we must address it immediately every single time in the moment. Use this prayer and use it consistently during the day when you become upset:

"Allow me to see clarity where I see upset. It is no longer about me."

Evening Soul Surgery

worry   stress   fear   insecurity

think too much   alone   upset   frustration

resentment   overwhelm   defensive   exhausted

hate   anxiety   addiction   codependency

inauthentic   dishonesty   disloyalty   apathy

give up   fakeness   depression   judgement

Circle any of the principles above that come to your mind. Write the things in your life based on the words circled that are still holding you hostage (even if it's a repeat from another entry).

_____

_____

_____

_____

_____

_____

_____

Upon completing the list use the following prayer to wipe your mind clean:

"Allow me to let go of what is upsetting me that I may be healed on the deepest level. Remove my difficulties that I may be present and of greater service."

(Initial)

By initialing you acknowledge that you lived one spiritually responsible day. What you did today is enough to change yourself which enough to change the world. Good job ☺

Daily Practice

Date: _____

Morning Intention

Today is the Day.
Today is all I have. Today is all I need.

"Free me from the bondage of self that I may live in the present and with authenticity. Allow me to be the person I am meant to be as a light shining in this world serving others still in need."

playful   creative   meaning   grateful   service

joyful   purpose   passion   inspiration

compassion   contentment   forgiveness

tolerance   loving   acceptance   intuition

integrity   honesty   loyalty   perseverance

authenticity   genuineness

Circle one of the principles above to bring in light for today. In the following lines write the actions or behaviors that you intend to do today to bring these concepts alive in your life. Keep it simple.

_____

_____

_____

_____

_____

_____

_____

Each day we have responsibilities that require our action. It is easy to add mountains to this list and squeeze out our spiritual life which is why we must let some of the list go. However, it would be dysfunctional to ignore basic responsibilities. The following list (no more than 5 items) is the simple version of what actually needs to be done today. Anything else accomplished will be a bonus but is intentionally dropped from expectation less it distract us from our spiritual work.

Responsibilities List:

➢ _____

_____

➢ _____

_____

➢ _____

_____

➢ _____

_____

➢ _____

_____

Clean as You Go

- Frustration

- Resentment

- Fear

- Insecurity

- Upset

When a situation triggers upset we must address it immediately every single time in the moment. Use this prayer and use it consistently during the day when you become upset:

"Allow me to see clarity where I see upset. It is no longer about me."

Evening Soul Surgery

worry   stress   fear   insecurity

think too much   alone   upset   frustration

resentment   overwhelm   defensive   exhausted

hate   anxiety   addiction   codependency

inauthentic   dishonesty   disloyalty   apathy

give up   fakeness   depression   judgement

Circle any of the principles above that come to your mind. Write the things in your life based on the words circled that are still holding you hostage (even if it's a repeat from another entry).

_____

_____

_____

_____

_____

_____

_____

_____

Upon completing the list use the following prayer to wipe your mind clean:

"Allow me to let go of what is upsetting me that I may be healed on the deepest level. Remove my difficulties that I may be present and of greater service."

_____

(Initial)

By initialing you acknowledge that you lived one spiritually responsible day. What you did today is enough to change yourself which enough to change the world. Good job ☺

Daily Practice

Date: _____

Morning Intention

Today is the Day.
Today is all I have. Today is all I need.

"Free me from the bondage of self that I may live in the present and with authenticity. Allow me to be the person I am meant to be as a light shining in this world serving others still in need."

playful   creative   meaning   grateful   service

joyful   purpose   passion   inspiration

compassion   contentment   forgiveness

tolerance   loving   acceptance   intuition

integrity   honesty   loyalty   perseverance

authenticity   genuineness

Circle one of the principles above to bring in light for today. In the following lines write the actions or behaviors that you intend to do today to bring these concepts alive in your life. Keep it simple.

_____

_____

_____

_____

_____

_____

_____

Each day we have responsibilities that require our action. It is easy to add mountains to this list and squeeze out our spiritual life which is why we must let some of the list go. However, it would be dysfunctional to ignore basic responsibilities. The following list (no more than 5 items) is the simple version of what actually needs to be done today. Anything else accomplished will be a bonus but is intentionally dropped from expectation less it distract us from our spiritual work.

Responsibilities List:

➤ _____

_____

➤ _____

_____

➤ _____

_____

➤ _____

_____

➤ _____

_____

Clean as You Go

- Frustration
- Resentment
- Fear
- Insecurity
- Upset

When a situation triggers upset we must address it immediately every single time in the moment. Use this prayer and use it consistently during the day when you become upset:

"Allow me to see clarity where I see upset. It is no longer about me."

Evening Soul Surgery

worry   stress   fear   insecurity

think too much   alone   upset   frustration

resentment   overwhelm   defensive   exhausted

hate   anxiety   addiction   codependency

inauthentic   dishonesty   disloyalty   apathy

give up   fakeness   depression   judgement

Circle any of the principles above that come to your mind. Write the things in your life based on the words circled that are still holding you hostage (even if it's a repeat from another entry).

_____

_____

_____

_____

_____

_____

_____

Upon completing the list use the following prayer to wipe your mind clean:

"Allow me to let go of what is upsetting me that I may be healed on the deepest level. Remove my difficulties that I may be present and of greater service."

———————

(Initial)

By initialing you acknowledge that you lived one spiritually responsible day. What you did today is enough to change yourself which enough to change the world. Good job ☺

Daily Practice

Date: _____

<u>Morning Intention</u>

Today is the Day.
Today is all I have. Today is all I need.

"Free me from the bondage of self that I may live in the present and with authenticity. Allow me to be the person I am meant to be as a light shining in this world serving others still in need."

playful   creative   meaning   grateful   service
joyful   purpose   passion   inspiration
compassion   contentment   forgiveness
tolerance   loving   acceptance   intuition
integrity   honesty   loyalty   perseverance
authenticity   genuineness

Circle one of the principles above to bring in light for today. In the following lines write the actions or behaviors that you intend to do today to bring these concepts alive in your life. Keep it simple.

_____

_____

_____

_____

_____

_____

_____

Each day we have responsibilities that require our action. It is easy to add mountains to this list and squeeze out our spiritual life which is why we must let some of the list go. However, it would be dysfunctional to ignore basic responsibilities. The following list (no more than 5 items) is the simple version of what actually needs to be done today. Anything else accomplished will be a bonus but is intentionally dropped from expectation less it distract us from our spiritual work.

Responsibilities List:

➢ _____

  _____

➢ _____

  _____

➢ _____

  _____

➢ _____

  _____

➢ _____

  _____

Clean as You Go

- Frustration
- Resentment
- Fear
- Insecurity
- Upset

When a situation triggers upset we must address it immediately every single time in the moment. Use this prayer and use it consistently during the day when you become upset:

"Allow me to see clarity where I see upset. It is no longer about me."

Evening Soul Surgery

worry   stress   fear   insecurity

think too much   alone   upset   frustration

resentment   overwhelm   defensive   exhausted

hate   anxiety   addiction   codependency

inauthentic   dishonesty   disloyalty   apathy

give up   fakeness   depression   judgement

Circle any of the principles above that come to your mind. Write the things in your life based on the words circled that are still holding you hostage (even if it's a repeat from another entry).

_____

_____

_____

_____

_____

_____

_____

_____

Upon completing the list use the following prayer to wipe your mind clean:

"Allow me to let go of what is upsetting me that I may be healed on the deepest level. Remove my difficulties that I may be present and of greater service."

(Initial)

By initialing you acknowledge that you lived one spiritually responsible day. What you did today is enough to change yourself which enough to change the world. Good job ☺

Daily Practice

Date: _____

Morning Intention

Today is the Day.
Today is all I have. Today is all I need.

"Free me from the bondage of self that I may live in the present and with authenticity. Allow me to be the person I am meant to be as a light shining in this world serving others still in need."

playful   creative   meaning   grateful   service

joyful   purpose   passion   inspiration

compassion   contentment   forgiveness

tolerance   loving   acceptance   intuition

integrity   honesty   loyalty   perseverance

authenticity   genuineness

Circle one of the principles above to bring in light for today. In the following lines write the actions or behaviors that you intend to do today to bring these concepts alive in your life. Keep it simple.

_____

_____

_____

_____

_____

_____

_____

Each day we have responsibilities that require our action. It is easy to add mountains to this list and squeeze out our spiritual life which is why we must let some of the list go. However, it would be dysfunctional to ignore basic responsibilities. The following list (no more than 5 items) is the simple version of what actually needs to be done today. Anything else accomplished will be a bonus but is intentionally dropped from expectation less it distract us from our spiritual work.

Responsibilities List:

➤ _____

_____

➤ _____

_____

➤ _____

_____

➤ _____

_____

➤ _____

_____

Clean as You Go

- Frustration
- Resentment
- Fear
- Insecurity
- Upset

When a situation triggers upset we must address it immediately every single time in the moment. Use this prayer and use it consistently during the day when you become upset:

"Allow me to see clarity where I see upset. It is no longer about me."

Evening Soul Surgery

worry   stress   fear   insecurity

think too much   alone   upset   frustration

resentment   overwhelm   defensive exhausted

hate   anxiety   addiction   codependency

inauthentic   dishonesty   disloyalty   apathy

give up   fakeness   depression   judgement

Circle any of the principles above that come to your mind. Write the things in your life based on the words circled that are still holding you hostage (even if it's a repeat from another entry).

_____

_____

_____

_____

_____

_____

_____

Upon completing the list use the following prayer to wipe your mind clean:

"Allow me to let go of what is upsetting me that I may be healed on the deepest level. Remove my difficulties that I may be present and of greater service."

_____

(Initial)

By initialing you acknowledge that you lived one spiritually responsible day. What you did today is enough to change yourself which enough to change the world. Good job ☺

Daily Practice

Date: _____

Morning Intention

Today is the Day.
Today is all I have. Today is all I need.

"Free me from the bondage of self that I may live in the present and with authenticity. Allow me to be the person I am meant to be as a light shining in this world serving others still in need."

playful   creative   meaning   grateful   service
joyful   purpose   passion   inspiration
compassion   contentment   forgiveness
tolerance   loving   acceptance   intuition
integrity   honesty   loyalty   perseverance
authenticity   genuineness

Circle one of the principles above to bring in light for today. In the following lines write the actions or behaviors that you intend to do today to bring these concepts alive in your life. Keep it simple.

_____

_____

_____

_____

_____

_____

_____

Each day we have responsibilities that require our action. It is easy to add mountains to this list and squeeze out our spiritual life which is why we must let some of the list go. However, it would be dysfunctional to ignore basic responsibilities. The following list (no more than 5 items) is the simple version of what actually needs to be done today. Anything else accomplished will be a bonus but is intentionally dropped from expectation less it distract us from our spiritual work.

Responsibilities List:

➤ _____

_____

➤ _____

_____

➤ _____

_____

➤ _____

_____

➤ _____

_____

Clean as You Go

- Frustration

- Resentment

- Fear

- Insecurity

- Upset

When a situation triggers upset we must address it immediately every single time in the moment. Use this prayer and use it consistently during the day when you become upset:

"Allow me to see clarity where I see upset. It is no longer about me."

Evening Soul Surgery

worry   stress   fear   insecurity

think too much   alone   upset   frustration

resentment   overwhelm   defensive   exhausted

hate   anxiety   addiction   codependency

inauthentic   dishonesty   disloyalty   apathy

give up   fakeness   depression   judgement

Circle any of the principles above that come to your mind. Write the things in your life based on the words circled that are still holding you hostage (even if it's a repeat from another entry).

_____

_____

_____

_____

_____

_____

_____

Upon completing the list use the following prayer to wipe your mind clean:

"Allow me to let go of what is upsetting me that I may be healed on the deepest level. Remove my difficulties that I may be present and of greater service."

(Initial)

By initialing you acknowledge that you lived one spiritually responsible day. What you did today is enough to change yourself which enough to change the world. Good job ☺

Daily Practice

Date: _____

Morning Intention

Today is the Day.
Today is all I have. Today is all I need.

"Free me from the bondage of self that I may live in the present and with authenticity. Allow me to be the person I am meant to be as a light shining in this world serving others still in need."

playful   creative   meaning   grateful   service
joyful   purpose   passion   inspiration
compassion   contentment   forgiveness
tolerance   loving   acceptance   intuition
integrity   honesty   loyalty   perseverance
authenticity   genuineness

Circle one of the principles above to bring in light for today. In the following lines write the actions or behaviors that you intend to do today to bring these concepts alive in your life. Keep it simple.

_____

_____

_____

_____

_____

_____

_____

Each day we have responsibilities that require our action. It is easy to add mountains to this list and squeeze out our spiritual life which is why we must let some of the list go. However, it would be dysfunctional to ignore basic responsibilities. The following list (no more than 5 items) is the simple version of what actually needs to be done today. Anything else accomplished will be a bonus but is intentionally dropped from expectation less it distract us from our spiritual work.

Responsibilities List:

➢ _____

_____

➢ _____

_____

➢ _____

_____

➢ _____

_____

➢ _____

_____

Clean as You Go

- Frustration
- Resentment
- Fear
- Insecurity
- Upset

When a situation triggers upset we must address it immediately every single time in the moment. Use this prayer and use it consistently during the day when you become upset:

"Allow me to see clarity where I see upset. It is no longer about me."

Evening Soul Surgery

worry   stress   fear   insecurity

think too much   alone   upset   frustration

resentment   overwhelm   defensive   exhausted

hate   anxiety   addiction   codependency

inauthentic   dishonesty   disloyalty   apathy

give up   fakeness   depression   judgement

Circle any of the principles above that come to your mind. Write the things in your life based on the words circled that are still holding you hostage (even if it's a repeat from another entry).

_____

_____

_____

_____

_____

_____

_____

Upon completing the list use the following prayer to wipe your mind clean:

"Allow me to let go of what is upsetting me that I may be healed on the deepest level. Remove my difficulties that I may be present and of greater service."

(Initial)

By initialing you acknowledge that you lived one spiritually responsible day. What you did today is enough to change yourself which enough to change the world. Good job ☺

Daily Practice

Date: _____

Morning Intention

Today is the Day.
Today is all I have. Today is all I need.

"Free me from the bondage of self that I may live in the present and with authenticity. Allow me to be the person I am meant to be as a light shining in this world serving others still in need."

playful   creative   meaning   grateful   service
joyful   purpose   passion   inspiration
compassion   contentment   forgiveness
tolerance   loving   acceptance   intuition
integrity   honesty   loyalty   perseverance
authenticity   genuineness

Circle one of the principles above to bring in light for today. In the following lines write the actions or behaviors that you intend to do today to bring these concepts alive in your life. Keep it simple.

_____

_____

_____

_____

_____

_____

_____

_____

Each day we have responsibilities that require our action. It is easy to add mountains to this list and squeeze out our spiritual life which is why we must let some of the list go. However, it would be dysfunctional to ignore basic responsibilities. The following list (no more than 5 items) is the simple version of what actually needs to be done today. Anything else accomplished will be a bonus but is intentionally dropped from expectation less it distract us from our spiritual work.

Responsibilities List:

➢ _____

_____

➢ _____

_____

➢ _____

_____

➢ _____

_____

➢ _____

_____

Clean as You Go

- Frustration
- Resentment
- Fear
- Insecurity
- Upset

When a situation triggers upset we must address it immediately every single time in the moment. Use this prayer and use it consistently during the day when you become upset:

"Allow me to see clarity where I see upset. It is no longer about me."

Evening Soul Surgery

worry   stress   fear   insecurity

think too much   alone   upset   frustration

resentment   overwhelm   defensive   exhausted

hate   anxiety   addiction   codependency

inauthentic   dishonesty   disloyalty   apathy

give up   fakeness   depression   judgement

Circle any of the principles above that come to your mind. Write the things in your life based on the words circled that are still holding you hostage (even if it's a repeat from another entry).

_____

_____

_____

_____

_____

_____

_____

Upon completing the list use the following prayer to wipe your mind clean:

"Allow me to let go of what is upsetting me that I may be healed on the deepest level. Remove my difficulties that I may be present and of greater service."

_____

(Initial)

By initialing you acknowledge that you lived one spiritually responsible day. What you did today is enough to change yourself which enough to change the world. Good job ☺

Daily Practice

Date: _____

Morning Intention

Today is the Day.
Today is all I have. Today is all I need.

"Free me from the bondage of self that I may live in the present and with authenticity. Allow me to be the person I am meant to be as a light shining in this world serving others still in need."

playful   creative   meaning   grateful   service

joyful   purpose   passion   inspiration

compassion   contentment   forgiveness

tolerance   loving   acceptance   intuition

integrity   honesty   loyalty   perseverance

authenticity   genuineness

Circle one of the principles above to bring in light for today. In the following lines write the actions or behaviors that you intend to do today to bring these concepts alive in your life. Keep it simple.

_____

_____

_____

_____

_____

_____

_____

Each day we have responsibilities that require our action. It is easy to add mountains to this list and squeeze out our spiritual life which is why we must let some of the list go. However, it would be dysfunctional to ignore basic responsibilities. The following list (no more than 5 items) is the simple version of what actually needs to be done today. Anything else accomplished will be a bonus but is intentionally dropped from expectation less it distract us from our spiritual work.

Responsibilities List:

> _____

_____

> _____

_____

> _____

_____

> _____

_____

> _____

_____

Clean as You Go

- Frustration
- Resentment
- Fear
- Insecurity
- Upset

When a situation triggers upset we must address it immediately every single time in the moment. Use this prayer and use it consistently during the day when you become upset:

"Allow me to see clarity where I see upset. It is no longer about me."

Evening Soul Surgery

worry   stress   fear   insecurity

think too much   alone   upset   frustration

resentment   overwhelm   defensive   exhausted

hate   anxiety   addiction   codependency

inauthentic   dishonesty   disloyalty   apathy

give up   fakeness   depression   judgement

Circle any of the principles above that come to your mind. Write the things in your life based on the words circled that are still holding you hostage (even if it's a repeat from another entry).

_____

_____

_____

_____

_____

_____

_____

Upon completing the list use the following prayer to wipe your mind clean:

"Allow me to let go of what is upsetting me that I may be healed on the deepest level. Remove my difficulties that I may be present and of greater service."

_____

(Initial)

By initialing you acknowledge that you lived one spiritually responsible day. What you did today is enough to change yourself which enough to change the world. Good job ☺

Daily Practice

Date: _____

Morning Intention

Today is the Day.
Today is all I have. Today is all I need.

"Free me from the bondage of self that I may live in the present and with authenticity. Allow me to be the person I am meant to be as a light shining in this world serving others still in need."

playful   creative   meaning   grateful service
joyful   purpose   passion inspiration
compassion   contentment   forgiveness
tolerance   loving   acceptance   intuition
integrity   honesty   loyalty   perseverance
authenticity   genuineness

Circle one of the principles above to bring in light for today. In the following lines write the actions or behaviors that you intend to do today to bring these concepts alive in your life. Keep it simple.

_____

_____

_____

_____

_____

_____

_____

_____

Each day we have responsibilities that require our action. It is easy to add mountains to this list and squeeze out our spiritual life which is why we must let some of the list go. However, it would be dysfunctional to ignore basic responsibilities. The following list (no more than 5 items) is the simple version of what actually needs to be done today. Anything else accomplished will be a bonus but is intentionally dropped from expectation less it distract us from our spiritual work.

Responsibilities List:

➢ _____

_____

➢ _____

_____

➢ _____

_____

➢ _____

_____

➢ _____

_____

Clean as You Go

- Frustration

- Resentment

- Fear

- Insecurity

- Upset

When a situation triggers upset we must address it immediately every single time in the moment. Use this prayer and use it consistently during the day when you become upset:

"Allow me to see clarity where I see upset. It is no longer about me."

Evening Soul Surgery

worry   stress   fear   insecurity

think too much   alone   upset   frustration

resentment   overwhelm   defensive   exhausted

hate   anxiety   addiction   codependency

inauthentic   dishonesty   disloyalty   apathy

give up   fakeness   depression   judgement

Circle any of the principles above that come to your mind. Write the things in your life based on the words circled that are still holding you hostage (even if it's a repeat from another entry).

_____

_____

_____

_____

_____

_____

_____

Upon completing the list use the following prayer to wipe your mind clean:

"Allow me to let go of what is upsetting me that I may be healed on the deepest level. Remove my difficulties that I may be present and of greater service."

(Initial)

By initialing you acknowledge that you lived one spiritually responsible day. What you did today is enough to change yourself which enough to change the world. Good job ☺

Congratulations.

You have completed the 30 day workbook. It is advised that you continue the Daily Practice in one form or another. Continue to refine the cultivation of hardships as lessons that we integrate into our lives each time owning our sense of authenticity, passion, and service.

Live with intention.
Stay inspired.

ABOUT THE AUTHOR

John Cassone
MS, MSAOM, PhD, LAc, DAOM(c)

Dr. Cassone began his career over twenty years ago using lifestyle modifications and nutritional therapies with a goal of reducing chronic illness and ultimately improving the quality of life for those he served. Today, he holds two master's degrees in health sciences, a doctorate in nutrition, and is currently pursuing a second doctorate in integrative medicine (DAOM). He has effectively treated patients from all over the world. Dr. Cassone is a licensed **Primary Care** provider in the state of California.

In 2000, Dr. Cassone opened Range of Motion, a fitness center located in San Pedro, California which has grown to become a South Bay leader in fitness & wellness. The main practice is located in Temecula, California however he is able to treat patients anywhere using modern technologies and internet conferencing.

drcassone.com

Branch Vs Root Treatment

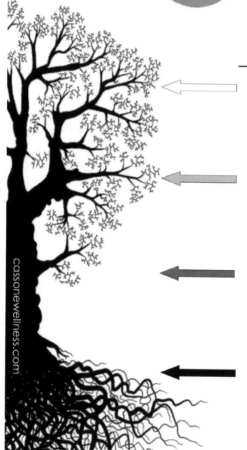

Symptom
- symptoms only; no investigation of cause

Function
- assessment of biological systems causing symptoms

Emotion
- understanding how emotional states affect body functions

Spirit
- approach to life causing unnecessary fear, conflict, depression

cassonewellness.com